Mount...

Water Hole

Sandy or
Gravelly Flats

Arroyo or Wash

Desert Places

To Paul for your steadfast support—Dorothy

The Wild Wonders Series is supported in part by the
Lloyd David and Carlye Cannon Wattis Foundation.

The animals and plants illustrated in this book are typical of the
Sonoran Desert of North America and have been reviewed and
approved by scientists at the Denver Museum of Natural History.

We would like to thank Dr. Charles Preston, Curator of Ornithology
at the Denver Museum of Natural History, for reviewing this book.
His help and input at all stages of this project were invaluable.

Book design by Jill Soukup

International Standard Book Number 1-57098-174-4
Library of Congress Catalog Card Number 97-068061

Published by the Denver Museum of Natural History Press
2001 Colorado Boulevard, Denver, Colorado 80205
in cooperation with Roberts Rinehart Publishers
5455 Spine Road, Boulder, Colorado 80301
(303) 530-4400

Distributed in the U.K. and Ireland by
Roberts Rinehart Publishers
Trinity House, Charleston Road
Dublin 6, Ireland

Distributed to the trade in the U.S. and Canada by Publishers
Group West

Printed in China

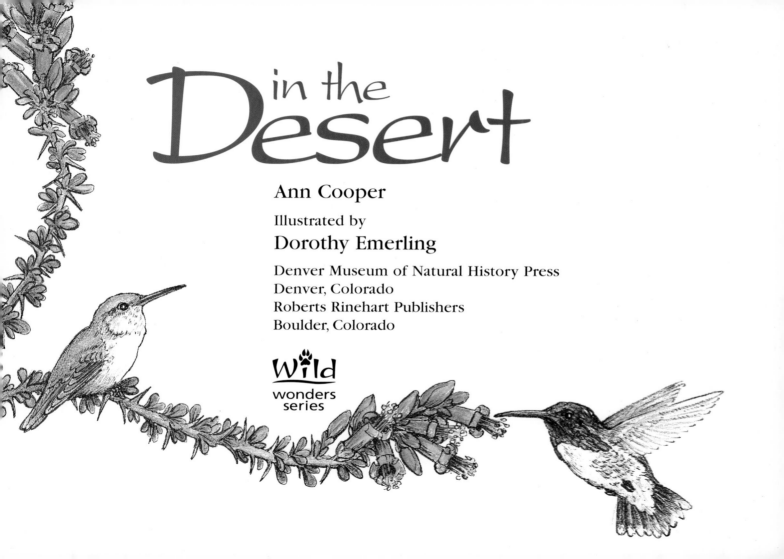

in the Desert

Ann Cooper

Illustrated by

Dorothy Emerling

Denver Museum of Natural History Press
Denver, Colorado
Roberts Rinehart Publishers
Boulder, Colorado

W**i**ld
wonders
series

What Makes a Desert?

Does heat make a desert?
At noon, heat rises in wavy shimmers from the desert
floor. The sun scorches down from a cloudless sky.
A lizard flicks from a cactus patch. It sprints across
baking gravel—toes barely touching—and vanishes
into a hole. A vulture soars above a distant peak.
Nothing else moves. It is too hot . . . but not always.
Desert nights may be cool—even cold. No clouds
blanket the earth and keep it warm. Daytime heat
is soon lost. In winter, snow may drift down. *Brrr!*
Heat does not make a desert.

Does emptiness make a desert?
Some deserts are nothing but miles of sand. Few plants
grow there. Few animals live in such harsh places. But some
deserts are magical gardens full of life. They grow cactus
forests, spiny bushes and trees, and, after rain, carpets of
wildflowers. Many animals live in these deserts and use
the plants—prickles and all—for food, shelter, and homes.
These deserts are not empty!

Scarce rain makes a desert.
A summer storm might bring flash floods. More often,
it brings only a few fat splats of rain in the dust. Deserts
get less than ten inches of rain a year. Some years,
no rain falls at all. All plants and animals that live
here adapt to life with little water.

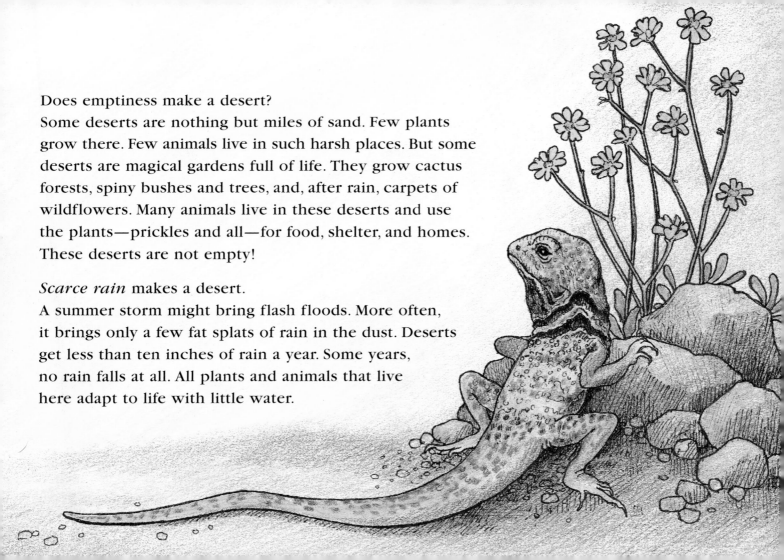

Day Shift, Night Shift

Tap-tap-tap echoed across the flats. Woodpecker was carving a new home in a tall saguaro. He pecked until he had made a deep, boot-shaped hole. Woodpecker's mate laid four white eggs there. Night and day, they tended the eggs. One morning, a whipsnake slithered up the saguaro's fat trunk between rows of prickles. Woodpecker flew at the snake, pecking wildly. Another day, Hawk landed on the top arm, but he only wanted to eat the mouse he'd caught.

One night, Elf Owl returned from his winter in Mexico. He flew from one saguaro to another, hole-hunting. He peeked into a fine, scabby cavity. *Churrrr,* Woodpecker's mate squawked, waking suddenly. She stabbed at the shape at her door. *Yip-yip-yip,* Owl called, flying to a hole higher up the trunk. It was a fine home-hole—empty—with few prickles to snag his feathers!

Time passed. Each day, Woodpecker brought insects to his chicks. Owl snoozed in a thorny tree while his mate sat on two white eggs. Each dusk, the woodpeckers roosted. Owl hunted for moths, beetles, crickets, and scorpions to bring back to his mate. Woodpecker and Owl were neighbors—day shift and night shift—but rarely saw one another.

Saguaro Cities

Homes for All

Woodpeckers chip new nest holes each year. Old holes are in great demand! Elf owls, martins, kestrels, mice, and snakes all use them. Hawks often build their huge stick nests in a saguaro's upper arms.

Elf Owls

Elf owls are the size of sparrows. They catch venomous scorpions and break the scorpions' stinger-tails before feeding the scorpions to their owlets. The owl shown is life-size.

Seed Helpers

Hovering bats sip nectar from saguaro flowers—and get their noses dusted with pollen! The pollen brushes off on the next flower the bat visits and helps make seeds.

Keep Your Cool

A nest hole in a saguaro is cool in the heat of day and warm on chilly nights. The saguaro's thick flesh offers insulation and a wind shield.

Enemies

Snakes sometimes slither up the prickly trunks of saguaros to steal eggs or baby birds from cavity nests left unguarded.

Supermarket?

Nearly everyone "shops" at the saguaro. Doves eat the saguaro's buds, fruit, and seeds. Hummingbirds zip in to sip sweet nectar. Insects come for anything they can eat: nectar, pollen, and juicy flesh. Other birds fly in for insect fast-food.

Juicy Fruit. Yum!

When saguaro fruit ripens and falls, deer, coyotes, javelinas, kangaroo rats, ground squirrels, mice, and other animals feast.

Desert Boots

Saguaro flesh is squashy like a melon. A hard scab soon grows over pecked places to keep the saguaro's juice in. When a saguaro dies and falls, the scabby nest holes—desert boots—are the last to rot.

Jackrabbit's Run

Jackrabbit peeped out from a clump of prickly pear. His whiskers twitched as he sniffed the cool morning. He turned his ears this way and that, listening. All quiet! He hopped, loppity-lop, to the edge of the arroyo in search of food. He nibbled a blade or two of grass, lolloped a lazy step or two, and nibbled again. Food was easy to find this year after good winter rains.

Hoppity-hop. Jackrabbit snipped a daisy with his sharp front teeth. *Crack!* A twig snapped. Jackrabbit froze, the daisy still in his mouth. He was still hungry, but he was ready to run.

At the first sight of Coyote, Jackrabbit leaped in the air, then raced off in a wild zigzag across the flats. Coyote loped after him. Jackrabbit's heart pumped *thumpety-thump.* He bounced as if his long legs were made of rubber. He was hot, so-o hot. He risked a quick look behind him. Coyote was far away, eating. Jackrabbit ran a bit farther, just in case. Then he flopped down in the shelter of a thorny bush to cool off and catch his breath.

Eyes Front?

With its large, wide-set eyes, a jackrabbit can watch for enemies in all directions as it eats.

Cool Ears

Enormous ears are a jackrabbit's air-conditioning. Warm blood flows through the thin ears and loses heat to the air. That's how jackrabbits cool their bodies in desert heat.

Food

Jackrabbits eat grasses, wildflowers, cactus fruits, and the leaves, pods, and bark of shrubs and trees—especially mesquite.

Sprint Champions?

Jackrabbits can run as fast as 40 miles an hour, but not for long! They soon get tired. They can long-jump 15 feet.

Family Life

A jackrabbit makes an aboveground, fur-lined nest in a clump of grass or a hollow cactus patch.

Mother jackrabbits have several litters (families) a year. Each litter has three to six babies. They can run around a few hours after birth.

Rabbit or Hare?

In spite of their name, jackrabbits are hares, not rabbits. Hares are large, with long ears and legs. Their furry babies are born ready to run. Rabbits are small. They give birth to blind, nearly naked babies.

Enemies

Coyotes, foxes, bobcats, snakes, eagles, and hawks hunt jackrabbits. Some Harris' hawks hunt in pairs, diving at desert cottontails and "jacks" until the prey animals get tired and confused. The hawks dive and catch them.

Scat-Eater

A jackrabbit may pass small pellets of moist scat (droppings), then eat them again. That way, it gets a second chance to digest more vitamins and take back more water.

Scatter!

Quail clucked softly as she and her mate hurried along the arroyo. This year she had so many chicks to watch, she didn't know where to turn. *Plink-plink,* she called, trying to keep the family together. The chicks scurried this way and that, pecking seeds and fruits. One chick darted after a small lizard, curious. Poof! The lizard vanished down its hole. Another chick startled a hummingbird, which zoomed away from a bright red penstemon.

Quail cluck-clucked again, as if to say "Hurry up, youngsters." She was anxious to get to the water hole on this hot day, so she and the family could drink. At last, the chicks followed, like tiny fuzz balls with legs. They passed a jackrabbit, who went on munching. Quails did not concern him.

A dark shadow suddenly swept across the ground. *Ke-eer, ke-eer* cries came from the sky. Mother Quail and her chicks scattered into the underbrush. A ground squirrel interrupted its peaceful dust bath and popped down its hole. A spiny lizard scurried under a rock. It was as if the arroyo were suddenly empty of life. Mother Quail waited . . . and waited . . . until the hawk had flown far across the flats. Then she called *plink-plink* to reunite her family.

Quail Facts

Nests

Quail use dead leaves, twigs, and grass to build shallow nests, usually on the ground. A female lays ten to twelve eggs. Two females may lay their eggs in the same nest. What a crowd! The feathered chicks hatch ready to run, but cannot fly for a week to ten days.

Voices

Quail have far-carrying voices. The male's main call (*pu-kwaa-ke*) in the heat of the day is a well-known desert sound.

Drinking

Some desert birds, such as quail and doves, like to drink every day. The quail usually walk to a nearby water hole. The doves may fly many miles. People have discovered water in the desert by watching the direction of the doves' regular morning and evening flights.

Enemies

Coyotes, foxes, and hawks prey on quail. Snakes and lizards may take eggs and chicks from nests.

Eggs for Brunch

Gila monsters are the only poisonous lizards in the United States. They eat baby mice and rabbits, and the eggs and chicks of ground-nesting birds such as quail. These large lizards spend much time underground, living off fat stored in their tails.

Egg Timers

More flowers bloom in rainy years. Quail find plenty of food and lay many eggs. The hatched chicks find lots of food.

In dry years, the few flowers soon shrivel. Quail must eat less-favored plants, including a clover that keeps them from laying so many eggs. That's handy! Fewer chicks hatch when food is scarce!

Little Fox

Little Fox yawned and stretched. Her sister and brothers were asleep in a heap, taking too much space. The den felt cramped. Little Fox scrabbled up the tunnel—the way her mother went. She stopped . . . listened . . . set off again, not sure what she would find. Then she came to the sandy front door. She tilted her pointy nose high to sniff the evening.

Bumpity-bump! Her brothers shoved past and began chasing and tumbling. She joined in, growling little growls, then racing away. One brother tried to grab her fur, but she was too fast. She frisked away. A "thing" sat on a rocky ledge. Little Fox froze. She sniffed and watched, then took a few steps toward it. The lizard-thing—a chuckwalla—scuttled into a crack and puffed up its body. Little Fox jumped back, startled.

When Father arrived from the hunt with something in his mouth, Little Fox rushed back to see. Her brothers pushed and jostled and fought over the rat. Each one wanted a mouthful. They were so busy squabbling, they didn't see Mother Fox catch a cactus mouse. When Mother dropped the mouse, Little Fox pounced. She shook the dead mouse hard and tossed it high in the air, practicing hunting.

Fox Facts

Kit Foxes

Kit foxes, the smallest foxes in the desert, are the size of small cats. Their ears are large. Their hairy paws help them run in loose sand.

Family Life

Kit foxes give birth to three or four young in spring. The helpless babies stay in the den for several weeks, drinking milk from their mother. Later, both parents bring food until the young are ready to leave the den and hunt for themselves.

Food and Drink

Kit foxes eat kangaroo rats, ground squirrels, mice, baby rabbits, small birds, lizards, and insects. They get most of the water they need from their food.

Play

Foxes play to make their bodies strong, to practice balance, and to learn hunting skills.

They use special signs—flat ears, drooping tails, and bared teeth—to "talk" to each other. Each fox learns to know by signs if another fox is playing or fighting for real.

Enemies

Coyotes, mountain lions, bobcats, and owls may catch kit foxes.

Dens

Foxes live in dens with lots of tunnels and many ways in and out. The dens are about two feet belowground. The fox may dig the whole den, or enlarge and remodel a kangaroo rat's mound.

Neighbors

Ringtails leave their canyon dens to hunt mice. Scorpions crawl out from under rocks or fallen cactus skeletons to catch insects. Male tarantulas set out in search of a mate. Night is a busy time!

Sssnake

All day, Snake rested, curled in an old badger hole,
barely moving. At sunset, a fiery glow backlit the
cactus forest. Then the sky faded to lavender.
Snake slipped out of his hole, forked tongue
flicking. He stretched out on the gravel, soaking
up heat. Then silently, with a ripple of his belly
muscles, he slithered away to hunt.

He flicked his tongue in and out, testing the air for the scent of mouse. Round a prickly pear patch, under a smoke bush, over the woody skeleton of a dead cactus—Snake's body flowed. He crossed a faint trail leading to a mound of holes. His tongue tasted rodent on the air. Snake coiled his long body and waited.

A pocket mouse scurried out of a small hole. It scampered a short way and stopped to gather seeds. Snake felt the tiny vibrations of the mouse's footsteps. He waited. The mouse scuttled a few steps closer and stopped again. Snake could feel the warmth from the mouse's body. He knew which way to strike.

Who-huh-who-who-who. A shadowy shape swooped from high above. Snake rattled his tail once and slithered down a nearby hole. He could not wait for mice here when Owl was about.

About Rattlesnakes

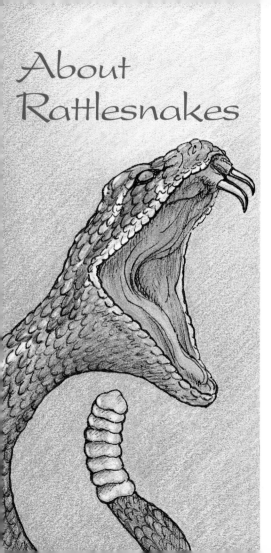

Venom

A rattlesnake kills prey with venom, which drips from slits in the side of the fangs, not the tips. Fangs hinge flat into the snake's mouth when they are not in use. If a fang breaks, a new one takes its place.

Snakes do not chew food. They open their mouths ENORMOUSLY wide and swallow prey whole.

Tongues

A snake's flicking forked tongue gathers scents from the air and brings them back to special taste-testing cells in its mouth.

Pit Viper

A rattlesnake has small pits (holes) on its head that sense heat. The snake feels a mouse's warmth from a foot away and can strike accurately in total darkness.

Babies

Most reptiles lay eggs in the soil. Rattlesnakes give birth to live young.

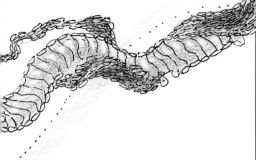

Shedding

A snake rubs its nose on the ground to loosen its papery skin. It slithers forward and leaves the inside-out skin behind.

Hot and Cold

Snakes cannot make warmth in their bodies. They bask in the sun to warm up. They move to shade, or underground, to cool down. If a snake gets too hot, it dies.

Rattles

A rattlesnake has dry, horny segments on its tail, which it rattles when it feels threatened. The snake grows an extra rattle segment each time it sheds its skin.

You cannot tell how old a snake is by counting rattles. It may gain several new rattles each year, but some rattles break or wear away.

Food

Snakes eat mice, rats, kangaroo rats, voles, rabbits, birds and birds' eggs, and many other animals. Some snakes even eat other snakes.

Enemies

Hawks, roadrunners, owls, and kingsnakes prey on small rattlesnakes. Large rattlers have few enemies.

Fast-Food, Please

Wren built his best nest in the middle of a spiny cholla. The nest was as big as a football and had a strong roof to keep out sun and rain. The only door was a hole leading to a dark, narrow tunnel. While his mate sat on their eggs, Wren built another nest. It was for his next family—and a night roost, too.

At last, four chicks hatched. Each day they grew hungrier. With no rest from dawn to dusk, Wren and his mate gleaned food for them. Time and again, Wren flew from the mesquite tree with juicy grubs, diving into the entrance tunnel and popping out again like a cork from a bottle. Time and again, *chee, chee, chee,* the chicks squawked for more. Would they never be full?

As the sun sank behind the western hills in a rosy glow, Wren flew home with a final grasshopper. What was that din? His mate was fluttering around their nest scolding, *tsuu, tsuu, tsuu.* A brown shape scuttled over the prickly branches, then dropped to the ground. It was Packrat with a cholla joint in its mouth, scurrying home to add to its enormous nest.

About Cactus Wrens

Families

A cactus wren lays three to six pink, cinnamon-speckled eggs. The eggs hatch in about sixteen days. The young fly about three weeks later. A mother wren has two families a year.

Nests Galore

Wrens make several nests. They use the extra nests as night roosts and snug winter hideouts. Extra nests may also distract the wrens' enemies from the "real" nest full of eggs or chicks.

Home Wrecker

Curve-billed thrashers also make their nests in cholla bushes. They do not like wrens as close neighbors and destroy nearby wrens' nests. Thrashers build open, cup-shaped nests. On hot days, females sit on their eggs to keep them cool with bird-shade!

Woodrats

Also known as packrats, these rodents build big nests under rocks or in cactus bushes. They use sticks, cactus joints, and sometimes shiny things they find—pop-tops, foil, and spoons!

Food

Wrens eat beetles, bugs, grasshoppers, ants, and some seeds. They rarely drink, but get the water they need from juicy insects.

What a Din!

If a snake comes near a wren's nest, the wrens make a ratchety racket. They fly from bush to bush, scolding and fussing, until the snake moves on.

Other wrens in nearby territories do the same. Harsh chatter follows the snake as it squirms across the desert!

Enemies

Snakes, hawks, and roadrunners may take eggs, young, or even adult cactus wrens—if they can find them among the prickles!

Little Pig, Little Pig...

Javelina and her babies spent the day resting in the shade of a mesquite thicket. The whole band lazed there. It was so-o hot! All around, flowers were dry and withered. The grass had turned crisp and brown. Even the puddle around the freshwater spring had shrunk. There was scarcely any water to drink, let alone mud to wallow in.

As evening came, the band set off to find food. Javelina snuffled in the edge of the dry wash, dropping to her knees to snout out roots to eat. Then she trotted to a patch of prickly pear cactus. *Munch, crunch.* She bit into the spiny pads and ate the sweet flesh and prickles, too. It was juicy and watery, good food for a dry day.

Over the mountains, towering clouds had gathered. *Zap!* Rumbling filled the air. Javelina's babies tried to run under her belly for safety. But she and the rest of the band were already trotting toward the rocky hillside, grunting and woofing as they went. A wash was no place to be when a storm was brewing! The young javelinas scurried to catch up, trotting as fast as their little hooves could carry them.

Javelina Facts

Water! Water!

Javelinas need water every day. They drink at tanks (pools in rock that hold water between rains), water holes, or springs. Finding water is part of the day's work.

They may even drink at "coyote wells." These are scraped holes in a dry-looking stream where a coyote has dug to reach water under the surface. Any water is precious in the desert!

Names

Javelinas are also called collared peccaries, for their collars of pale-colored fur.

Family Life

A female javelina goes away by herself when her one or two babies are born. She rejoins her band (family group) after a few days.

Enemies

Mountain lions, coyotes, and bobcats may prey on javelinas, and eagles may catch the young.

Escape!

When the band is disturbed, javelinas scatter in all directions—fast. They grunt and yip to find each other and get back together again.

What a Smell!

Javelinas nuzzle each other with their snouts and chins to spread musk (a smelly oil) from a gland near their tail. They can tell by smell if a javelina is a stranger or belongs to their band.

Food

Javelinas eat roots, tubers, insect grubs, lizards, toads, snakes, and the eggs of ground-nesting birds. They also like cactus pads, fruits, and mesquite beans.

Toads Galore

Spadefoot toads live for months underground, waiting for rain. Then they dig out and croak for mates.

Eggs—tadpoles—toads! It all happens in a hurry, before the desert ponds dry up again.

Lizard's Tale

Warm from the morning sun, Lizard was ready for a meal. He scuttled down from the rock where he had been basking. Zip! He flicked his tongue and caught a spider. *Gulp.* It was gone in no time. Zip! A grasshopper. Zap! An unwary beetle. This was a good, buggy place to live.

Lizard took no notice of the horned lizard that lived near the anthill. It just lurked there, eating ants. But when a whiptail hurried from a hole, that was different! This was *his* home and *his* food! He bobbed his head once, twice. He stiffened his front legs, hunched his back, and made his body look as big as possible. The whiptail flicked its tongue at a beetle. *Crunch!* Lizard ran toward the whiptail, his striped tail flicking. He pumped up and down on his thin front legs. He swelled his throat, as if to say "I'm the boss."

Just as the whiptail flicked away to safety, Lizard heard a scrabbling behind him. He looked around. Roadrunner—bird of the stabbing beak—was dashing toward him. Lizard flicked away as fast as he could go, his tail waving wildly. Ouch! He felt a tweak! But he kept on running.

About Lizards

Tails

If a predator snatches a lizard's long tail, the tail breaks. The lizard's enemy gets a wiggling tail section. The lizard gains time to escape. The tail grows back, but is often crooked.

Roadrunner

A roadrunner *can* fly, but it usually runs about on the ground to catch lizards, snakes, and insects. It hunts large prey—more than it can swallow—and may hang around for hours with a lizard or snake dangling from its beak. The bird sometimes gets only the lizard's tail!

Hot and Cold

A lizard can't make heat in its body. It is always as warm or as cold as its surroundings. It dashes from sun to shade to keep its body heat right.

Lots of Lizards

Lizards are the easiest animals to see in the desert, because they are active by day, and there are lots of them.

Fancy Toes

Fringe-toed lizards can scurry across loose sand and not sink in, because they have large, fringed feet. They escape from enemies by using their feet to "swim" down into the sand.

Leaping Lizards!

The collared lizard runs at about sixteen miles an hour. At this speed, it may run on its hind legs. It also jumps from rock to rock as it hunts for spiders, insects, and other lizards to eat.

Enemies

Lizards are hunters *and* hunted. Snakes, scorpions, and many birds prey on lizards. Even lizards prey on other lizards!

Shedding

Like snakes, lizards shed their skin when they need to grow. The whitish skin often comes off in shreds. The lizard eats the skin, because it contains material too nutritious to waste.

Kangaroo Rat's Night Out

Kangaroo Rat plugged his door with earth. Snug in his burrow, he slept all day. When night came, he heard pounding on his roof. Rain was falling. He stayed home. He didn't like to get his fur wet. The only bath he liked to take was a dust bath!

Next night, Kangaroo Rat scratched open his door. He popped his nose and whiskers out. The air felt fresh and steamy. He hopped—*boing! boing!* on his back feet—toward the arroyo and stopped. Water rushed and tumbled, scouring chunks from the bank where he usually gathered seeds. Grinding sounds hurt his ears. With a flip of his tufted tail, he turned—*boing!*—and hopped to high ground.

The rain had knocked many fruits and seeds to the ground. Kangaroo Rat leaped this way and that, stuffing his cheek pouches. He had never seen so many seeds in one place! He bounced to his burrow to unload, pushing the seeds out of his cheeks with his front paws. Then he bounced out for more, taking an extra-long leap over a hairy tarantula wandering across the path. He almost landed on a beetle. Everyone was on the move tonight!

Kangaroo Rat Facts

Families

A female kangaroo rat's two to three babies are born in a grass-lined nest deep in a burrow. At birth they have no fur. Their eyes open in two weeks. They are fully grown at five to six weeks, but stay with their mother for a few months.

Long Jumper

Kangaroo rats hop about on their large hind legs, using their tails to steer and balance. To escape enemies, they zigzag wildly and leap as far as ten feet in one jump.

Water Saver

A kangaroo rat never needs to drink. Its body cells make almost all the water it needs as they turn food into energy. It gets some water from plants, insects, and dry seeds it eats.

A kangaroo rat's body is built to save water. The rat's urine is pasty, not liquid. Scat is solid. As the rat breathes out through its long and twisty nasal tubes, each breath cools and dries.

Senses

A kangaroo rat's eyes are set high and wide, for an all-around view. Its night vision is good. It hears well, especially low sounds of owls and rattlesnakes, and the *thump-thumping* of another kangaroo rat drumming a warning with its hind feet.

Pockets

A kangaroo rat's fur-lined cheek pouches open at the front (near the bottom teeth) and are separate from the mouth. A kangaroo rat stuffs about a teaspoonful of seeds into each pouch, then hops back to its hole to eat in safety or store the seeds for later.

Flash Floods

Heavy rain cannot soak into the baked desert. Water rushes down the arroyos, tumbling things in its path. Some small animals drown. Later, scavengers eat them.

Enemies

Coyotes, kit foxes, gray foxes, badgers, skunks, owls, and snakes prey on kangaroo rats.

Animals All Around

Each prickly cactus patch, rocky outcrop, and shady bush may shelter countless creatures. Anywhere you go, there are more animals around than you see. Which of these other desert animals did you find as you read the story?

Horned Lizards

These well-camouflaged spiny lizards lie in wait for ants and other small insects. When attacked, they squirt blood from their eyes. (It's scary, but harmless!) They are also called horny toads, because of their toady shape, but they are reptiles and scaly, not warty like toads.

Turkey Vultures

These birds make a V-shape with their wings as they soar high above. They scavenge carrion (dead animals).

Grasshopper Mice

These fierce predators eat insects, spiders, scorpions, and other mice. They howl like tiny wolves to warn other grasshopper mice away from their home territory.

Chuckwallas

When threatened, these vegetarian lizards hide in rock crevices. They wedge themselves in by gulping air to puff up their bodies.

Scorpions

These night-hunters eat spiders, insects, and small mammals. They catch prey with pincer claws, and subdue struggling prey with venom from a stinger tail. They can go months without eating!

Did You Find?

Bat
Bobcat
Badger
Coyote
Ringtail
Deer
Great horned owl
Hawk
Dove
Hummingbird
Collared lizard
Gecko
Whipsnake
  Ants, beetles, spiders, butterflies, and crickets

Around the Clock

There are no rules to tell animals when to be active and when to sleep. For some animals, it depends on the time of year. It depends on how cold it is by night and how hot and dry by day. The story animals fit roughly like this:

▲ Nocturnal (nighttime) animals keep cool and hunt for food under cover of darkness.

▲ The "in-between" animals are active mostly from late afternoon to early morning, but they may be out and about by day depending on the season.

▲ Diurnal (daytime) animals keep going, hot or not! Most of them stay in the shade.

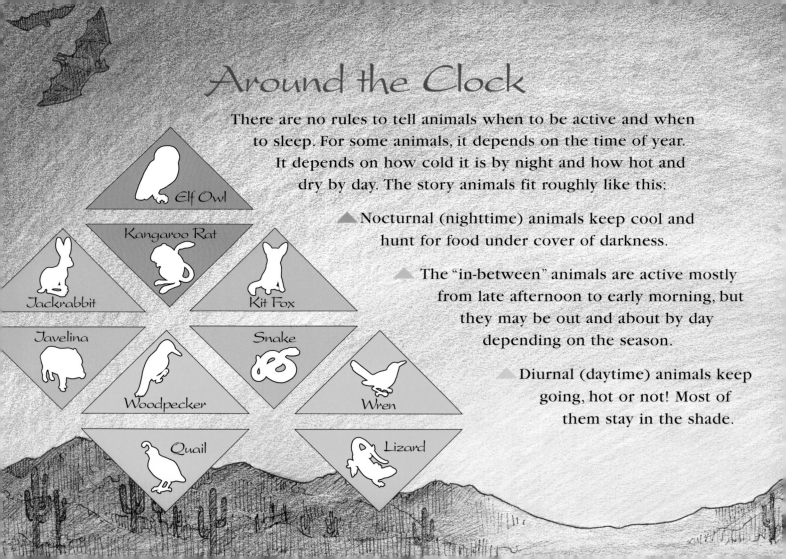

Elf Owl

Kangaroo Rat

Jackrabbit

Kit Fox

Javelina

Snake

Woodpecker

Wren

Quail

Lizard

Down Below

On hot-hot days, holes stay cooler than "up top." Here are seven animals that spend lots of time in the cool safety of underground: ant, badger, lizard, spider, kangaroo rat, beetle, snake.

Tracks

Did you notice tracks and marks on some pages? They are life-size. Measure them with your hand to test the size of the animals' feet.

Treasure Maps

Front map: Find a saguaro where Woodpecker might have carved a nest. Find the water hole where Quail's family drank.

Back map: Which animal uses the smallest space? Which animals visit the spring? Which animal has a den near the rocky outcrops?

Water! Water!

Desert animals get water any way they can. Do you remember which animal used which way?
• Which got water from juicy prickly pear pads?
• Which made water as it turned food to energy?
• Which got enough water from the insects it ate?
• Which visited the water hole to drink?

Links of Life

Who would choose to live in a desert?
Water is scarce. Rains do not always come in time.
The summer sun dries wildflowers to a crisp.
Trees and bushes drop their leaves to save water.
Tall saguaros become skinnier and more pleated
by the week as their water stores are used up.
You might think this is a terrible place to live—
yet it is the only home the desert animals know.

What if it *is* hot?
Under the summer sun, the desert may be
almost silent, except for the distant
pu-kwaa-ke call of a quail.

But under the stars, the desert comes alive. The air is loud with countless grunts and rattles, thumps and rustles, whines and buzzes. This is a busy habitat.

What if it *is* dry?
The desert animals are used to lack of rain. They drink when they can. They make the most of water in their food. Their bodies are adapted to use water sparingly.

Hot or cold, wet or dry, the animals get on with their busy lives—trying to find food, trying to raise young, trying to survive. All of them, from the smallest beetle on a cactus pad to the hawk on high, are important strands in the web of desert life.